GOD BLESS THE

WRITTEN BY

CHRISTOPHER YEATES

© Gresham Books 2016
Published by Gresham Books Limited
The Carriage House, Ningwood Manor, Ningwood
Isle of Wight PO30 4NJ

ISBN 978 0 946095 80 3

GOD BLESS THE QUEEN

WRITTEN BY
CHRISTOPHER YEATES

COVER AND ILLUSTRATIONS BY
MATTHEW RICE

PUBLISHED BY
GRESHAM BOOKS

With grateful thanks to Hong and Kathleen Yeoh for sharing the values of faith and duty with so many.

God Bless the Queen
What's inside

HISTORY IN THE MAKING

We are living in a very exciting period of royal history. On September 9th 2015, Queen Elizabeth became Britain's longest reigning monarch, overtaking the record held by her great great grandmother, Queen Victoria. Since her coronation in 1953, our Queen has become a loved and much respected figurehead at home and abroad, patiently steering the UK through six decades of incredible change. For a little perspective, try to imagine a world without internet, without mobile phones, where everyday air travel was a thing of the future, and where man had not yet landed on the moon. Twelve UK prime ministers, twelve US presidents, thirty corgis, and a number of astonishing hats later, Queen Elizabeth is showing no signs of slowing, and the book in your hands is your very own guide to her life, duties and interests, and to the evolving importance of the monarchy in our society today.

THE LIFE OF A PRINCESS

1926 was an important year for famous births. Queen Elizabeth, or Princess Elizabeth of York (as she was known back then), wasn't the only famous person born in 1926. Keeping her company was David Attenborough and Marilyn Monroe who have both, in rather different ways, become stars of the screen. It was also, believe it or not, an uncommonly good year for bears. Michael Bond, creator of Paddington Bear, was born in January, and in October, A.A. Milne first published

Winnie-the-Pooh. The most important day of that year, however, was April 21st, when Elizabeth Alexandra Mary was born in Mayfair, London, to the Duke and Duchess of York. Perhaps you think it's a bit odd that we celebrate the Queen's birthday in June, when she was born in April. Luckily, there are two very good reasons for this. Firstly, it's more likely to be sunny (or at least not raining) in the summer month of June. Secondly, it means the Queen gets two lots of presents. Bear this little trick in mind for your own birthday next year!

EDUCATING ELIZABETH

It might surprise you to learn that Lilibet, as her family called her, didn't go to school. Don't get jealous too quickly, though. Even though Lilibet

and her sister, Margaret Rose, were educated at home, they still had to study French, art, music, religious studies, mathematics, and history. What's more, if you think teachers are strict, imagine being taught by two of the sternest men in the country – the Archbishop of Canterbury, and your own dad, the King of England! Happily, if the girls were good (which wasn't always, especially in Margaret's case), they got to learn more enjoyable skills such as dancing, singing and horse riding.

ROYALS AT WAR

In 1939, at the outbreak of World War II, the King and Queen sent Elizabeth and Margaret to live in Windsor Castle, away from London which was suffering the worst of the bombing. Nonetheless, the sisters got very used to rolling out of bed and into an air-raid shelter when the sirens rang out, signalling an approaching attack. If you had been alive at that time, you may have been among the three million children evacuated from their homes, and sent to live in places around the country which were less likely to be bombed. As you can imagine, it would have been a scary time. Understanding this, Princess Elizabeth, aged fourteen, made the first of her famous radio broadcasts, encouraging the children of Britain by telling them 'that in the end, all will be well; for God will care for us and give us victory and peace.' How would you have felt, hearing these words?

A few years later, in 1945 when she was 18 years old, the Princess joined the Auxiliary Territorial Service. This was the women's branch of the British Army during the war. For a few months before the end of the fighting, Elizabeth learned to drive and repair heavy vehicles. This made her the first female Royal Family member to be a full-time active member of the Services. Today, as the Queen, she is the Head of the Armed Forces, and meets regularly with the Chief of Defence to make sure the UK stays protected.

World War II also affected Princess Elizabeth's wedding to Lieutenant Philip Mountbatten (now the Duke of Edinburgh). The years after the war were tough, and just like every other young bride at the time, Elizabeth had to collect coupons to save up for her wedding dress. The couple were married in Westminster Abbey on November 21st, 1947.

The QUEEN'S WEDDING

AN UNEXPECTED QUEEN

In the early years of her life, nobody expected Princess Elizabeth ever to become Queen. This was because her uncle Edward, Prince of Wales, was the heir to the throne and there was no good reason why her father should have become king. At a young age, the Princess was a keen artist, swimmer, and member of the Girl Guides. She has said that had Royal life not beckoned, she would have liked to become a vet or a ballerina. Being the Queen of millions of people around the world probably seemed a long way off. And yet that is exactly what happened in the space of a few short years.

In 1936, Elizabeth's grandfather, King George V, passed away. His son, who became King Edward VIII, was King for only 326 days before deciding to give up the throne in order to marry the woman he loved, an American named Wallis Simpson. In those days it was unthinkable for the King to marry a lady who had been divorced, so there was no option but to give up the throne. Romantic, perhaps, but not ideal for his brother Bertie (Elizabeth's father), who reluctantly became King George VI in 1937. His reluctance was in part due to a speech impediment, a problem he eventually overcame. There's an excellent film called 'The King's Speech', if you want to know more about it. George became a popular King, symbolising Britain's fortitude during the war against the Nazis. But in February 1952, after a lengthy illness, he died peacefully in his sleep and Princess Elizabeth, in Kenya at the time of his death, became Queen Elizabeth II.

⚜ THE CORONATION ⚜

On June 2nd, 1953, Elizabeth's coronation at Westminster Abbey was the first in history to be watched on television. Today we expect to be able to watch anything and everything we want to, in colour and high-definition, either on TV or online. But watching the coronation in their own living rooms, even in black and white, would have been as new and exciting to people 63 years ago as talking robots would be to you today.

After 16 months of planning, 20 million people around the world watched the coronation, while three million people lined the streets of London to watch the two-mile long procession make its way towards Westminster Abbey. Many of these spectators had camped overnight in the rain to get the best view.

THE MONARCHY TODAY

A monarchy is where a King or Queen is Head of State. As you will
know, there have been many powerful Kings and Queens of the British
Isles in the last thousand years. When a King or Queen has lots of power
over the country and its people, we call this an executive monarchy.
When a King or Queen has only a little bit of power, we call this a
ceremonial monarchy.

Queen Elizabeth is a ceremonial Monarch. This is because, unlike
powerful rulers of history such as Henry VIII and Elizabeth I, who
were a law unto themselves, our Queen cannot make or enforce laws.
Instead, at least every five years, every adult in the country votes in an
election for whom they want to be Prime Minister. Technically, the
Prime Minister is more powerful than the Queen. We call this system
democracy, and it is generally considered to be the fairest way of
running a country. Democracy involves lots of people making decisions
about how the country is run, not just a small group of people (who
always seem to end up with more than everybody else). As soon as you
are eighteen years old, you will be able to vote in elections, and be a part
of this process.

A BIT OF GRISLY HISTORY

It is important to understand when and why the UK stopped having
an executive monarchy, and started having a ceremonial one. It comes
down to a contest between two ways of ruling a country: a Parliament

(which is democratic), or a Monarchy (which, traditionally, is not). This contest is precisely why we had the English Civil War (1642 – 1651). If you've ever been taught about this war, you'll know that it was a particularly grisly one, claiming the lives of over 200,000 people, and leading to King Charles I having his head lopped off by the Parliamentarians. Parliamentarians, as suggested by the name, wanted the country to be run by a Parliament, not the Monarchy, and they defeated the Royalists in battle. So after poor old Charles was deprived of his head, and his son driven into exile, England, Wales, Scotland and Ireland were run by Oliver Cromwell, who called himself a Lord Protector, and there was no King or Queen. We call this period of history, between 1653 and 1659, the Protectorate.

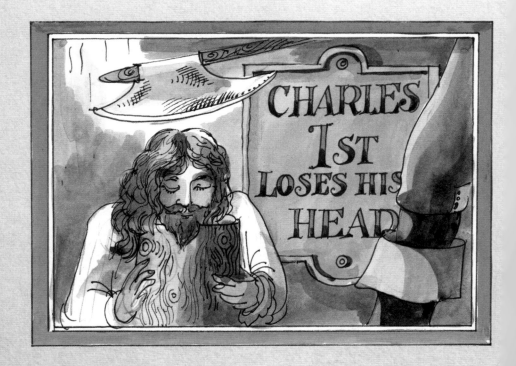

But the Protectorate was not to last. In 1660, Charles II, son of the executed Charles I, was crowned King, and the Monarchy was restored. Imaginatively, we call this period of history the Restoration. Charles II led a much happier life than his unfortunate father and died, in possession of both his head and the affections of at least a dozen mistresses, in 1685. His brother, James II, was crowned King. These were treacherous times, however, and Parliament encouraged an army from the Netherlands to invade England and take the throne. James fled, and his daughter Mary and her husband, who became William III, became King and Queen of England in 1689. Crucially, Parliament said that they could only become King and Queen if they signed a very important document: The Bill of Rights.

THE CONSTITUTION: VERY BRITISH VALUES

The Bill of Rights is so important because ever since it was signed, Kings and Queens of England have not been able to do whatever they pleased without asking Parliament first. It is one of the main reasons that the Monarchy today is largely ceremonial. Queen Elizabeth does not make any decisions which directly affect you or how the country is run. Instead, decisions about laws and the running of the country are made by politicians, mainly in Westminster, in London. The laws that Parliament makes apply to everybody equally. This is a nice change from earlier in history, when justice was often tougher on those who couldn't afford to bribe their way out of trouble!

Politicians today are not members of the Royal Family, they are not noblemen, and they do not automatically become politicians because of their families. They are elected democratically by people like you and me. In fact, there is nothing stopping you or anybody else becoming a politician and going to Westminster every day to help run the country as fairly and as smoothly as possible.

WHY DO WE HAVE A MONARCH AT ALL?

So, we have a ceremonial monarchy, which can't boss anybody around, and which must follow the British Constitution, a set of unwritten conventions. However, this does not mean that the Queen and the Royal Family are not important. In fact, they serve many useful and beneficial purposes in modern Britain. Queen Elizabeth is kept very busy by two sets of responsibilities: as Head of State, and as Head of Nation.

As Head of State, the Queen officially represents Britain to the rest of the world. She is our face, an important part of the UK's image – much like a mascot, but without the pom poms and breakdancing. In this role, Elizabeth has travelled all over the world for over 60 years, on hundreds of State Visits to other countries in order to strengthen friendships and improve economic ties. She also receives important guests here in the UK. Notable visitors have included the Japanese Emperor in 1971, Pope John Paul II in 1982, the American President Barack Obama and his wife Michelle, and the leaders of dozens of countries around the world. Being Head of State also involves carrying out political duties that help

Parliament to run fairly and smoothly; we'll take a look at these in the next section.

As Head of Nation, the Queen plays a less formal but still important role. The monarchy has always been a symbol of national identity, pride, and stability. Elizabeth has been particularly good at this unifying role, interacting with all sorts of people on a daily basis. Each year, the Queen and her family make around 3000 trips to different parts of the country in order to visit charities, events, hospitals, army bases, shopping centres, people's homes, and much besides. Further, Queen Elizabeth is patron of more than 600 charities and organizations, all of which benefit from her endorsement. The charitable work of the Queen and her family

The Queen is patron of the RNLI

has improved the lives of millions of people both in the UK and in developing nations around the world.

The Queen also has the power to bestow honours such as knighthoods upon people who have made an outstanding contribution to national life. Other awards are aimed specifically at young people. There is the Duke of Edinburgh Award scheme, for example, which challenges young people to develop special skills, help in their community, and go on exciting adventures. Another is the Queen's Young Leaders Awards, introduced in 2014.

HOW THE MONARCHY WORKS

The most important thing to know about the Queen in this respect is that she isn't allowed to take sides. She must remain what we call politically neutral, and not favour one political party over another. There are three political duties that the Queen must perform as Head of State:

1. When politicians have decided that a new law should be introduced, they show it to the Queen. It does not become a law until the Queen agrees to it – or gives her Royal Assent. This is usually what happens. In fact, the last time that a King or Queen did not give their assent to a new law being made was over 300 years ago. Queen Elizabeth has personally given Royal Assent to more than 3,500 Acts of Parliament.

2. Do you remember we said that every five years, we have an election to decide who is going to be the new Prime Minister? Because she cannot take sides, the Queen does not vote in the election. But when the votes have been counted, the Queen welcomes the new Prime Minister with a speech. This speech is given in the Houses of Parliament to every politician, and lets them begin the work of the next five years. We say that the speech opens Parliament.

3. The Queen has a special relationship with whoever is Prime Minister. Almost every Wednesday evening during her 63 years as Queen, Elizabeth has spent an hour in private discussion with

the Prime Minister about what is happening in the country. That's well over 3000 hours of talking, with 12 different Prime Ministers. Because of her longevity and experience, the Queen is a great source of wisdom for leaders, who value her advice and opinions.

1951–1955: . . . . Sir Winston Churchil

1955–1957: . . . . Sir Anthony Eden

1957–1963: . . . . Harold Macmillan

1963–1964: . . . . Sir Alec Douglas-Home

1964–1970/1974–1976: . . . . Harold Wilson

1970–1974: . . . . Edward Heath

1976–1979: . . . . James Callaghan

1979–1990: . . . . Margaret Thatcher

1990–1997: . . . . John Major

1997–2007: . . . . Tony Blair

2007–2010: . . . . Gordon Brown

2010– : . . . . David Cameron

THE UNION

Elizabeth is Queen of the United Kingdom, made up of England, Northern Ireland, Scotland and Wales. The centre of political power in the UK is in London, in the Houses of Parliament. However, since 1998, Northern Ireland, Scotland and Wales have each had their own Parliaments, or 'Assemblies' (not the school kind!) This means that they have a little more autonomy, or freedom, to make certain laws which apply to their own countries.

The national flag of the UK is the Union Flag (nicknamed the Union Jack), which is flown at all sorts of important national and international occasions such as State Visits and sports events. It flies, of course, during the Trooping of the Colour, an annual ceremony performed by the Household Cavalry to celebrate the Queen's official birthday. The Union Jack began as a red cross on a white background, the flag of England and St George, our dragon-slaying patron saint. When Scotland and Ireland became part of the UK (in 1270 and 1801 respectively), their flags were cleverly combined with England's to fashion the Union Jack that still flies today.

THE QUEEN AND UK LAW

We have already said that Queen Elizabeth is a ceremonial monarch, because she cannot directly make new laws, or punish people that break the law. Even so, she is still, rather grandly, considered the Fount of Justice. This name dates back to Anglo-Saxon times, when all-powerful executive monarchs acted as judge, jury, executioner, and everything in between when it came to serving up justice.

Today, because of documents like The Bill of Rights and the establishment of democracy, justice in the UK is carried out by the judiciary, who act in the Queen's name. Judiciary is the word we use to describe judges, who sit in courtrooms with big white wigs and tiny hammers and shout 'Order, Order!' when things get out of hand. In the interests of fairness, the judiciary is kept separate from the Government. Politicians can tell a police officer, or a soldier, what to do – but they cannot tell a judge what to do. In fact, nobody can tell a judge what to do, not even Queen Elizabeth – which means they have to be particularly wise and responsible!

THE QUEEN AND UK RELIGION

Elizabeth's other grand, rather enviable title is Defender of the Faith, which means that she is the leader of the Church of England. The first Defender of the Faith was Henry VIII. As I'm sure you're aware, Henry was the first to do a number of things, some of them good, some of them not so good. Being the first (and, indeed, the last) English monarch to break away from the Roman Catholic Church so that he could divorce Catherine of Aragon and marry Anne Boleyn, however, was probably the most significant of his trailblazing behaviours. By then, the Pope had already given Henry the title Defender of the Faith, and when he set up the Church of England, (the Anglican Church), the title stuck, and has been held by every King and Queen ever since. The Bill of Rights reinforces the royal bond with Anglicanism by stating that British monarchs must be fully confirmed members of the Church of England. Indeed, until 2013, they weren't even allowed to be married to a Roman Catholic.

As such, during her coronation back in 1953 (the one that was on TV), Queen Elizabeth swore an oath to protect the Church of England. Other ceremonial duties include appointing archbishops and bishops who, when chosen, swear an oath of allegiance to the Queen. And yet even though Elizabeth is head of the Church of England, the Royal Family are big supporters of religious tolerance and integration. In her Christmas message in 2004, the Queen said that, 'Everyone is our neighbour, no matter what race, creed or colour.' She meets frequently with religious leaders from Muslim, Hindu, Jewish, Sikh and other religious communities from all over the UK and the Commonwealth.

THE QUEEN AND THE COMMONWEALTH

At the beginning of the last century, Britain had the biggest empire in history: bigger than the Roman Empire, bigger than the Mongol Empire, bigger than the Empire of Alexander the Great. At one point, Queen Elizabeth's grandfather, King George V, was the ruler of 458 million people. At the time, that was about one in every five people on earth. Over the course of the last century, the Empire was slowly decolonized. This means that many of the countries within the Empire began to

govern themselves, rather than be under British rule. We say that these countries gained independence.

The British Empire is the reason that the Commonwealth exists. The Commonwealth is made up of 53 member states, many of which used to be part of the British Empire before they gained independence. Unlike the British Empire (which involved a lot of conquering and not a little bloodshed), nobody has to be part of the Commonwealth. It is a voluntary group of nations, and any nation can leave whenever they want to. Most want to stay, however, because of the social, cultural, and economic benefits of so many countries working together. The population of these countries is around two billion – or more than one in four people on earth.

Queen Elizabeth is head of the Commonwealth. There is a difference between a Commonwealth member (like India) and a Commonwealth realm (like Australia). Realms still recognise Elizabeth as their Queen; members do not. The 53 members of the Commonwealth include 16 realms. As head of the Commonwealth, Queen Elizabeth plays a symbolic and unifying role. During 200 trips, the Queen has personally visited every Commonwealth member except for two (Cameroon and Rwanda).

Some of the cultural values of the member states are represented on Commonwealth Day, which is held annually in March. Many different religions are celebrated in an inter-denominational service at Westminster Abbey, and Queen Elizabeth makes a speech to all of the Commonwealth members. On Commonwealth Day in 2013, Elizabeth

signed the Commonwealth Charter. This is an important document which highlights policies the group as a whole work towards achieving. These include democracy, human rights, peace and security, protecting the environment, education for all, and gender equality.

SYMBOLS OF POWER: ROYAL ICONS

The Crown Jewels is a collection of around 150 priceless ceremonial treasures that have been collected by Kings and Queens throughout history. They do not belong to Queen Elizabeth personally, but are part of the Royal Collection. You can go and see them at any time, stored safely in the Tower of London and guarded by the Yeomen Warders, better known as Beefeaters. Unfortunately, they have not always been so well cared for. In 1216, King John rather carelessly lost his Jewels in the quicksand of the Wash in East Anglia. A century later, Edward III sold his Crown Jewels in order to pay for an army he wanted. Worst of all, in 1649, Oliver Cromwell melted all of the Crown Jewels down and turned them into coins. Cromwell wasn't the Monarchy's biggest fan (he had Charles I executed, remember!), and cooking the Jewels was in keeping with his attempt to destroy the Monarchy for good. Luckily, some clever fellow had made records of what each item looked like, and so for Charles II's coronation in 1661, the Crown Jewels were replaced at a cost of £12,185, an enormous fortune in those days. These replacements were the beginning of the much larger collection on show in the Tower of London today.

Many of the Crown Jewels on display were used in Elizabeth's coronation in 1953. Items used in the coronation are special Jewels called regalia, and Britain is the only monarchy in Europe still to use regalia in coronation ceremonies. During her ceremony, Elizabeth was escorted to the Coronation Chair (or throne), which is over 700 years old. After she had taken the Coronation Oath, she was anointed by the Archbishop of Canterbury using the Ampulla and Anointing Spoon. The Ampulla is a golden flask in the shape of an eagle, which holds the holy oil. The Archbishop pours oil from the Ampulla into the Anointing Spoon, which is the oldest piece in the regalia. This is because it was the only item which survived when Cromwell destroyed the Jewels. With the oil from the Spoon, the Archbishop anointed Elizabeth on the hands, breast, and head, in a Biblical ritual that is thousands of years old. She was then dressed in ceremonial robes and presented with other items of regalia during what is called the investiture. These items include:

★ Spurs, made of solid gold. They represent knighthood and chivalry, and also the Monarch's role as Head of the Armed Forces.

★ The Sword of Offering, which is encrusted with 3,476 diamonds, rubies, emeralds, and sapphires.

★ The Coronation Ring, which was made for Queen Victoria's coronation in 1838. Unfortunately, the goldsmiths made the ring for the wrong finger, so that when the Archbishop forced it on during the ceremony, she couldn't get it off again!

★ The Sceptre with Cross, which has at its head the largest cut diamond in the world, called the Star of Africa. This Sceptre represents a Monarch's power as Head of State.

★ The Sceptre with Dove, which represents a Monarch's role as Head of the Church of England.

★ The St Edward's Crown, which was placed on Elizabeth's head at the moment of crowning.

THE QUEEN'S ANIMALS

A bit of horseplay - do you remember earlier when we said that Elizabeth would have liked to become a vet if she had not been Queen? Given her lifelong love of animals of all shapes and sizes, this isn't surprising; besides her pets, she is also the official owner of the UK's swans, and protects whales, dolphins, red squirrels and bats.

Elizabeth has owned more than 30 corgis during her reign. Many of these descended from Susan, a corgi who was given to Princess Elizabeth as an 18th birthday present. Three of her corgis, Monty, Willow and Holly, appeared in the 2012 Olympic opening ceremony when James Bond (played by Daniel Craig) arrived at Buckingham

Palace to fly the Queen to the stadium by helicopter. Looking after the pups is no laughing matter; a footman who once dared play a practical joke on the Queen's darlings by putting whisky in their water bowl was given a thorough dressing down!

The Queen's other great love is for horses. Her first pony, a Shetland called Peggy, was given to her by her grandfather King George V when she was 4 years old. The Queen greatly enjoys attending horseracing events, and is also interested in breeding. Her last riding horse was called Sanction, now buried in the grounds at Windsor Castle. Other pets have not been chosen by Her Majesty, but given to her as gifts from foreign countries. These have included jaguars, sloths, beavers, a crocodile, and a pair of pygmy hippopotami; none of these, however, are known for being particularly friendly towards snack-sized corgis, so were donated to London Zoo.

FOR THE COLLECTORS: STAMPS, COINS AND BANK NOTES

If you look at a coin, you'll see that one side bears the head of Queen Elizabeth. Coins in this country have shown the head of the reigning monarch for over 1000 years, a trend begun by Julius Caesar for propaganda purposes; it's a useful way of reminding your subjects how important you are. Of course, we hardly need reminding of this today, but the tradition continues, and the Royal Mint still produces limited edition coins for special events such as anniversaries and birthdays to add to the roughly 30 billion coins currently in circulation.

If you look at a bank note, you'll see that this too bears the image of Queen Elizabeth. And of course the Queen's head is also used on Royal Mail stamps. The image there has so far been reproduced on over 320 billion stamps!

 # THE NATIONAL ANTHEM

When you sing the National Anthem, the verses you are singing are over 300 years old, and have been sung by many millions of people before you. And they were all doing it for the same reason: to show respect, support and goodwill towards their monarch.

The version that we know and love today became popular in September 1745. King George's army had been defeated at the Battle of Prestonpans (near Edinburgh) by Prince Charles Edward Stuart, who wanted the throne for himself. Back in London, people were preparing themselves for an invasion, and spurring themselves into a fit of patriotic fervour with the rousing 'God Save the King'. It was first performed following a show at the Drury Lane Theatre, and other theatres were quick to follow suit. The only difference between what people sung in 1745 and the lyrics below is that we swap the word 'King' for 'Queen' – Queen Elizabeth might not be very impressed if we didn't.

God save our gracious Queen!
Long live our noble Queen!
God save the Queen!
Send her victorious,
Happy and glorious,
Long to reign over us,
God save the Queen.

Thy choicest gifts in store
On her be pleased to pour,
Long may she reign.
May she defend our laws,
And ever give us cause,
To sing with heart and voice,
God save the Queen.

And on that royal note, God bless the Queen!

A SERVICE OF THANKSGIVING TO COMMEMORATE THE 90TH BIRTHDAY OF HER MAJESTY QUEEN ELIZABETH II

Heavenly Father, who hast brought our gracious sovereign Queen Elizabeth to the completion of her ninetieth year, and dost gather her people in celebration of the same: grant that we, rejoicing before thee with thankful hearts, may ever be united in love and service to one another, and her kingdom flourish in prosperity and peace, through Jesus Christ our Lord.

All: Amen.

Over her long reign, Her Majesty, following the example set by Jesus Christ, has displayed the qualities of Wisdom, Service, Fortitude, and Tolerance. We give thanks for her long years of devoted service and pray that she might be an example to us all in our daily lives.

Reading

Happy is anyone who becomes wise—who comes to have understanding. There is more profit in it than there is in silver; it is worth more to you than gold. Wisdom is more valuable than jewels; nothing you could want can compare with it. Wisdom offers you long life, as well as wealth and honor. Wisdom can make your life pleasant and lead you safely through it. Those who become wise are happy; wisdom will give them life.

Proverbs 3. 13–18

All sing:

I vow to thee, my country, all earthly things above,
Entire and whole and perfect, the service of my love;
The love that asks no question, the love that stands the test,
That lays upon the altar the dearest and the best;
The love that never falters, the love that pays the price,
The love that makes undaunted the final sacrifice.

And there's another country, I've heard of long ago,
Most dear to them that love her, most great to them that know;
We may not count her armies, we may not see her King;
Her fortress is a faithful heart, her pride is suffering;
And soul by soul and silently her shining bounds increase,
And her ways are ways of gentleness, and all her paths are peace.

Cecil Spring-Rice (1859-1918)

Broadcasting to the world on 21st April, 1947, on her 21st birthday, the Queen said: "I declare before you all that my whole life, whether it be long or short, shall be devoted to your service and the service of our great imperial family to which we all belong… God help me to make good my vow, and God bless all of you who are willing to share in it".

Nearly 70 years later, in her 2015 Christmas broadcast, advocating resilience and faithful fortitude in the face of adversity, the Queen said: "The Gospel of John contains a verse of great hope, often read at Christmas carol services: 'The light shines in the darkness, and the darkness has not overcome it' … Despite being displaced and persecuted throughout his short life, Christ's unchanging message was not one of revenge or violence but simply that we should love one another."

All sing:

And did those feet in ancient time
Walk upon England's mountain green?
And was the holy Lamb of God
On England's pleasant pastures seen?
And did the countenance divine
Shine forth upon our clouded hills?
And was Jerusalem builded here
Among those dark satanic mills?

Bring me my bow of burning gold!
Bring me my arrows of desire!
Bring me my spear! O clouds, unfold!
Bring me my chariot of fire!
I will not cease from mental fight,

Nor shall my sword sleep in my hand,
Till we have built Jerusalem
In England's green and pleasant land.

William Blake (1757-1827)

Queen Elizabeth's fortitude has been necessary in her private life, as well as for the public good; for she has had her fair share of personal adversity to overcome. It is not only, however, Jesus' death and resurrection which gives our Queen strength, but the Scripture more widely, for as she has been known to ask, "To what greater inspiration and counsel can we turn than to the imperishable truth to be found in this treasure house, the Bible?" We can all take inspiration from a message that preaches strength and faith, no matter how dark the road.

Reading

Let us give thanks to the God and Father of our Lord Jesus Christ, the merciful Father, the God from whom all help comes! He helps us in all our troubles, so that we are able to help others who have all kinds of troubles, using the same help that we ourselves have received from God. Just as we have a share in Christ's many sufferings, so also through Christ we share in God's great help. If we suffer, it is for your help and salvation; if we are helped, then you too are helped and given the strength to endure with patience the same sufferings that we also endure. So our hope in you is never shaken; we know that just as you share in our sufferings, you also share in the help we receive.

2 Corinthians 1. 3–7

The tradition of Royal Christmas broadcasts stretches back to 1932, and Queen Elizabeth has addressed the nation at the end of almost every year since her accession. Over the years, a set of themes has consistently recurred, showing them to be of particular importance to Her Majesty: the importance of family, her concern for the lonely, for the poor, for the welfare of children, for the Armed Forces, and for the people of the Commonwealth. This last is very close to the Queen's heart; she has warmly embraced the transformation during her reign of the British Empire into today's Commonwealth, over which she benignly presides as a mother figure to millions around the world. In her 2004 Christmas Message, the Queen advocated that we extend tolerance, respect and love to all people, not just those who happen to share our particular faith or background:

"For me, as a Christian, one of the most important of these teachings is contained in the parable of the Good Samaritan, when Jesus answers the question, 'Who is my neighbour?' It is a timeless story of a victim of a mugging who was ignored by his own countrymen but helped by a foreigner – and a despised foreigner at that. The implication drawn by Jesus is clear. Everyone is our neighbour, no matter what race, creed or colour. The need to look after a fellow human being is far more important than any cultural or religious differences."

Reading

"A man was going down from Jerusalem to Jericho, when he was attacked by robbers. They stripped him of his clothes, beat him and went away, leaving him half dead. A priest happened to be going down the same road, and when he saw the man, he passed by on the other side. So too, a Levite, when he came to the place and saw him, passed by on the other side. But a Samaritan, as he travelled, came where the man was; and when he saw him, he took pity on him. He went to him and bandaged his wounds, pouring on oil and wine. Then he put the man on his own donkey, brought him to an inn and took care of him. The next day he took out two denarii and gave them to the innkeeper. 'Look after him,' he said, 'and when I return, I will reimburse you for any extra expense you may have.'

"Which of these three do you think was a neighbour to the man who fell into the hands of robbers?"

The expert in the law replied, "The one who had mercy on him."

Jesus told him, "Go and do likewise."

Luke 10. 30–37

The example of tolerance and goodwill to all men and women that the Parable sets is one that the Queen has followed throughout her life. The fount of this principle of tolerance, integration and a 'joining of hearts' is one of the Great Commandments of Christianity: "Thou shalt love thy neighbour as thyself". If we all followed Her Majesty's example, as we celebrate her 90 glorious years, we would have a country, indeed a world, of Power and Praise – but also Wisdom, Service, Fortitude, and Tolerance.

The following prayers have been written for Her Majesty on her 90th birthday by pupils from Early Years Foundation Stage up to Year 6:

Let us pray.

> Almighty Lord, thank you for the wonderful country we live in. We pray for the Queen today, on her birthday. We thank her for the effort she puts in to make this country the best it can be and for the respect she shows to everyone's viewpoint. Help us to remember that Her Majesty always works hard for others and loves and respects her people. Long live the Queen!
> Lord in your mercy,

All: Hear our prayer.

> Gracious Father, we thank you for helping our Queen with her royal duties. Please bless and watch over her when she is in need, especially on her ninetieth birthday. We also ask that she may have a wonderful time today and in the future.
> Lord in your mercy,

All: Hear our prayer.

> Heavenly Father, we pray that the Queen lives on to help run our country well. We pray that she will keep on with all the things she does. Thank you that she can talk to normal people, not just the heads of state. Thank you that people can send letters to the Queen and she meets with the Prime Minister every Wednesday. Please help the Queen to rule our country, and we pray that everything the Queen does improves our country.
> Lord in your mercy,

All: Hear our prayer.

Dear Loving Father, we thank you for our wonderful Queen who takes so much time communicating with the world. We ask that she is truly appreciated for all that she does from state occasions to garden parties . We ask that you grant her a happy birthday.
Lord in your mercy,

All: **Hear our prayer.**

Almighty Father, thank you for our amazing Queen and everything she does such as giving our prizes, writing letters to people who turn 100 and organizing marvellous banquets.
Help us to be good followers of her Majesty.
Help us to celebrate her 90th birthday this year.
Long may she reign over us. God save our Queen.
Lord in your mercy,

All: **Hear our prayer.**

Dear God, thank you for all the work the Queen does. Please make her Majesty keep doing her jobs like giving awards and making friends with other great leaders like the President of the USA. Help her praise those who have done great work for charities like the Blue Cross. We hope she has a brilliant 90th birthday. Long live the Queen!
Lord in your mercy,

All: **Hear our prayer.**

Dear God, thank you for our Queen. Thank you for a leader who has made our brilliant rules to keep us safe. Please let the Queen continue living a long and happy life.
Lord in your mercy,

All: **Hear our prayer.**

Dear God, thank you for our Queen and her health. I ask you God to bless our Queen for her leadership and all the wonderful things she does for us.
Lord in your mercy,

All: **Hear our prayer.**

Dear God, let the Queen be given wisdom and glory, I hope she
will be healthy, and Happy Birthday to her.
Lord in your mercy,

All: **Hear our prayer.**

All sing:

God save our gracious Queen!
Long live our noble Queen!
God save the Queen!
Send her victorious,
Happy and glorious,
Long to reign over us,
God save the Queen.

Thy choicest gifts in store
On her be pleased to pour,
Long may she reign.
May she defend our laws,
And ever give us cause,
To sing with heart and voice,
God save the Queen.

Happy Birthday, Your Majesty.

All: **Amen.**

With grateful thanks to the staff and pupils of
St Peter's Eaton Square CE Primary School, London SW1W 0NL;
and to Hong and Kathleen Yeoh for making this publication possible,
and for sharing their values of faith and duty with so many.